Wildland Visions
Newfoundland and Labrador

Wildland Visions
Newfoundland and Labrador

DENNIS MINTY

BREAKWATER

Breakwater
100 Water Street
P.O. Box 2188
St. John's, NF
A1C 6E6

Cover and Endpaper Photos: Dennis Minty

Canadian Cataloguing in Publication Data

Minty, Dennis.

    Wildland visions

    ISBN 1-55081-029-4

1. Newfoundland -- Description and travel --
1981 -- Views.   I. Title.

FC2167.5.M56 1993   971.8'04'0222   C91-097713-5
F1122.8.M56 1993

Printed and bound in Hong Kong.

— Dedication —

I dedicate this book to my mother whose love of life is in these pictures.

— Peace of Mind —

I photograph what I love—the expanses and the details of this land that is my home. Their texture, colour, moods, and interconnectedness are my inspiration. The wondrous light that bathes them shapes what I see. With camera in hand, I slow down, stop, and become absorbed by my surroundings. This process gives me peace of mind like nothing else. In fact that's what these pictures are—my peace of mind.

I owe this place, Newfoundland and Labrador, a great debt. It has given me a quality of life that I suspect is unattainable, for me, anywhere else on earth. With this book, I pay tribute to my home.

— On the Water —

My supreme escape is to slip the mooring from my Twillingate-crafted, juniper-ribbed, fir-planked boat on a sunny summer day to poke in and out of the coves and between the islands of one of our radiant bays.

Each summer for the past decade my family has tented for a few weeks tucked in some out-of-the-way inlet. We bring all we need and devote ourselves to each other and the place in which we happen to be.

Every day possible, we get out on the water. We steal away from everyday affairs and tomorrow's worries. The present is what matters. The slice of the boat through the swell. The immensity of the sea and the thrusting, everlasting headlands. The steady rhythm of the cleansing landwash on exposed beaches. The sanctuary of deep, lonely inlets. The humour of the monochrome turrs and kodachrome puffins that bounce, rubber-breasted, across the breakers as they try to take flight. The sudden, heart-stopping whoosh of a blowing whale close alongside. The incredible royal blues of the sea and the more solemn azure of its sister sky. The black-green stunted conifers ekeing sustenance from the most inappropriate cracks and shelves of the cliffs. The tight, ancient tuckamores of the cliff tops offering essential shelter to the meeker flora back from the edge. I know we are very lucky to be able to witness all of this and I'm glad that most others choose not to.

Most days are topped off with a picnic of bread, cheese, molasses and indispensable peanut butter, convened on a big flat rock near the mouth of a chuckling brook. Rarely finding any need for speaking, we soak up the present like dry sponges immersed too infrequently in the juice of life.

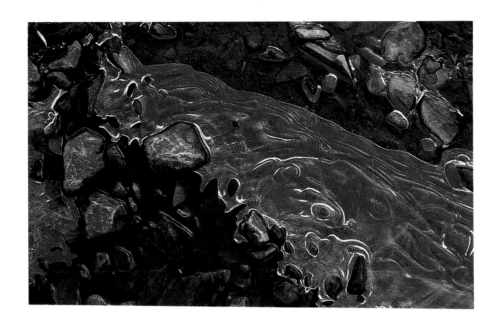

— Ice Amoeba —

A gravel track in late November is a unlikely spot to find beauty.
But the synergy of light, form and texture grabbed my eye just
before my six year old could transform it into muddy water and
icy shards.

— Eagles —

Almost every day we saw eagles along the shores of our British Harbour, Trinity Bay campsite. I wanted to make sure that my kids realized how precious these moments were, that most people would never see sights like this in their entire lives. But the looks in their faces told me I needn't be concerned. They knew.

— Big Sky —

Constrained by landscape or structure, the sky cannot express its expansiveness. Only over the water does it show itself fully to me. Never-ending, it wraps the earth's roundness beyond the horizons, beckoning my mind to stretch in kind. The only witness, I lie back and absorb the show. In one day the myriad changes both subtle and dramatic make human productions pale. It's a big feeling—this sense of the sky when afloat.

Perhaps we all long for a spiritualism of some kind. To many, it is in the form of religious constructs. To me, my cathedral is the big sky over open water.

— Torngats —

The scale of the Torngat Mountains is overwhelming. Jagged peaks nearly a mile high surge up from royal fjords that bring the cold, rich Labrador sea deep inland. Even in July, snow and ice cling to the deeply shaded northern faces. Glacierettes attest to the permanence of winter in valleys that rarely get a glimpse of the sun.

A person has no choice but to feel small here. The transience of human life is palpable. If the mountains could talk, I'm sure they would tell us that we humans really don't matter very much, that they will still be here in cold silence long after we have gone. But while we're here together, mountains and people, we would do well to understand from them that they are the essence of wildness, a tonic for those lucky enough to be in their midst.

— Bogs —

Crammed with life, bogs are the tropical jungles of northern Canada. Out of curiosity, I once counted fifteen different plants in a tabloid-sized area of one of these great sopping sponges.

So impressed with their diversity and charm, for Christmas one year I even gave my mother a piece of bog transplanted into a large aluminum roaster. She watered it and nurtured it through the winter to be rewarded with lemon bladderworts, beaujolais cranberries, and crimson pitcher plants. Admired by every visitor to our house, it sat proudly in front of our living room window for months, reminding us of the bounteous life under the snow. Mom, an avid berry picker and co-lover of bogs, was delighted.

— Reflections on Water —

Every pool I pass tugs at my eye. The light, sometimes as sharp as diamond points, at others as subtle as a day-dream, always casts back a surprise.

— Winter's Texture —

One clinging leaf remains after the raw winds of fall. Caught now in a shroud of ice, beautiful yet devastating, it evokes wintery thoughts.

Before you can enjoy Newfoundland's weather, you have to love the place. On this foundation you can tolerate the bad, which is often, and rejoice in the good which, when it comes, is truly worth a celebration

One winter day, cloaked in grey, may be bare underfoot. The next can be an elemental blast from the arctic, complete with waist-high drifts. The third can be so warm in the brilliant sun that you are mistakenly inspired to strip off.

When the wind stops (which is almost never), the stillness of the air makes you pause and wonder what is amiss. You are not sure if you are in the right place. Things feel suspended.

— Crow's Wing —

On a sublime, mild, fall day, when the air was rank with the tangy smell of dogberries and wet leaves, I was trekking the hills above my home in Carbonear. On a low hummock beside my path, there were signs of where a crow's day came to a rather violent end. Downy-grey tufts of feathers clung to the scarlet blueberry bushes but most of the carcass was gone. A lucky fox, I surmised. Perhaps the bird was a little less clever than the rest of his kin. The wings remained, luminescent in the autumn sun. I wondered how Walt Disney would explain this one to the Bambi crowd.

Although I revere nature as much as anyone can, I recognize that violence is a daily part of it. Our society protects itself from nature's raw edge by spending so little time outdoors. Instead, we choose to have nature supplied vicariously by some urban TV producer. The city-based interpretations of nature, and people's role in it, lean toward a pampered viewpoint. Blood on the snow disturbs the senses. As this TV-borne attitude permeates the countryside from its urban genesis, it affects those who love and use the land directly. Will the slow death of the hunting public be a good thing for nature? Are armchair nature lovers too isolated from its reality, buffered by the softened and filtered interpretations of others far away? The harvesters are at least outdoors experiencing it first hand.

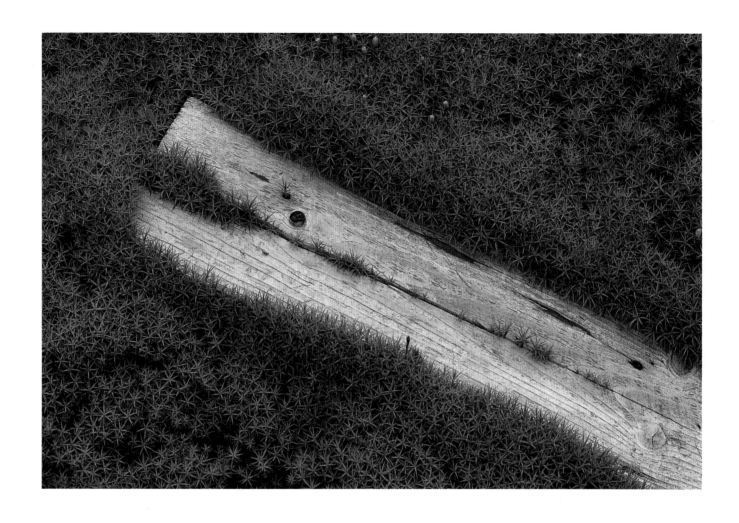

— Seeing up close —

Every day our preoccupation with routine causes most of us to pass images of outstanding beauty without ever taking notice. I do it too, except when I have camera in hand. Then I am open to them, and they are there in profusion.

The shapes and textures of our land are incredible if you take the time to look at them up close.

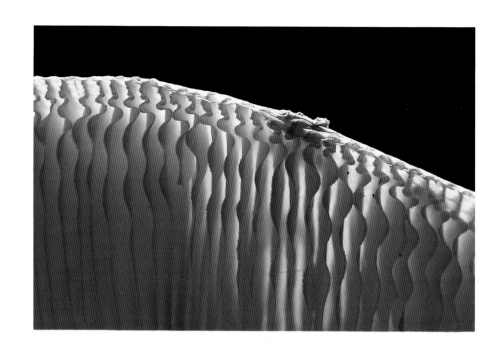

— Kittiwake Ledges —

Imagine catching your first glimpse of the world from a three inch ledge high above a sea pounding on craggy black rocks. It might give pause for thought. But no pause for thought here. Like an Italian family in crisis, all the folks are screaming. So it is for the kittiwake chick as it breaks from its shell.

Of course this is my view of the scene. The chick seems to take it all in stride.

In a few scattered places around our shores, thousands of seabirds cluster to breed and raise their young each year. Some of these colonies are the largest of their kind in the world, and we are their custodians.

— Islands —

Newfoundland Island is affectionately known as the "rock", but the "rocks" would be more accurate. Scattered along our coastline are families of smaller islands spawned from the mother rock. They are essential components of our unique character.

Under sail and muscle power, our boats used these islands as springboards to the fishing grounds. Every mile that a man didn't have to row was a precious saving of energy and time. So, in almost every cove that provided reasonable shelter, small communities sprang up. Churches were built, children were schooled, lives were lived.

After gasoline and diesel power, the islands lost some of their advantage. Resettlement policies encouraged people to leave them in favour of more concentrated services.

Now the islands are left largely unpeopled. The floors of old steamy kitchens, where gnarled hands slapped wooden tables in endless games of 120's, are tumbling seaward. The winds no longer find lines of clothes to dry. Scattered cemeteries with headstones askew and wild roses slowly spreading will be the last markers of a former time.

I hope the islands can remain this way, but recreational money is bringing ghetto blasters and broken beer bottles to their silent shores—brief bursts of obscenity in these isolated memorials. If only we could moderate the infiltration of our modern ways into these island sanctuaries. If only we could visit, pay respect to the life that once called these coves home,

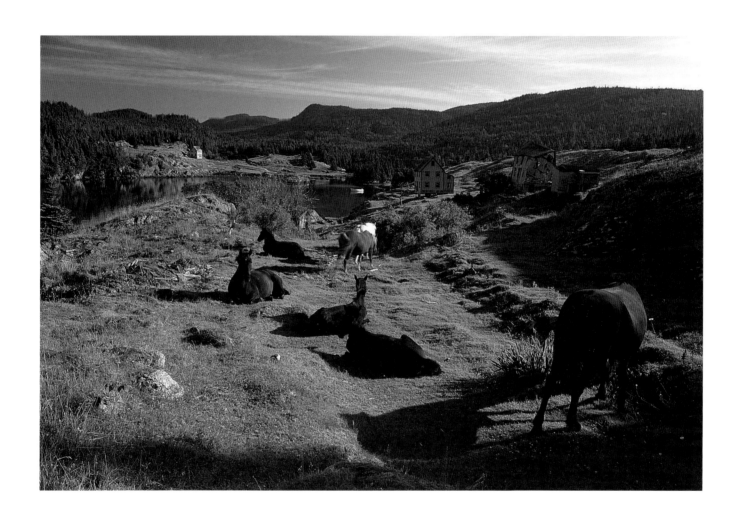

— Land Ownership —

How can we really 'own' land? It has existed from prehistory, and will exist long past the ends of our lives and that of our children. Rather than owners, we are only the temporary custodians of land—its stewards. We would be wise to exercise our stewardship well if we hope for our children to have an equal opportunity to exercise theirs.

— Bay du Nord —

The ecological prophets say that we have about twenty years left to protect our most vital natural areas. After that, it will be too late. As roads, transmission lines, mines, clear-cut logging, and other developments eat into our wilderness, by default we will have lost freedom to choose the best of wild Newfoundland and Labrador. Our economic agenda dictates that these developments occur, but our cultural and ecological well-being require that we also care for our wilderness.

For over fifteen years I have helped in the struggle to protect the places that really matter in the Province. Our progress has been painfully slow, but some gains have been made.

1990 was a landmark year. The Bay du Nord Wilderness Reserve was set aside—3500 square kilometres of Newfoundland's best unspoiled country. It has one of the finest wild rivers left on the island and an extensive network of huge lakes where canoe paddles can quietly dip in wilderness splendour; extensive barrenlands where several thousand woodland caribou thrive; thick, dark forests where the sound of a chain saw is alien; and vast wetlands where Canada geese congregate on the best breeding grounds of the island. It is a wild realm with an enduring landscape and fabric of life still largely unchanged since the first spirited pioneers ventured inland.

Our children, and theirs after them, will now have the opportunity to experience Newfoundland wilderness as has been available to us. Even if they do not travel through it, they can experience it vicariously through books, art, television or whatever new media become available. Just knowing that there are significantly large areas where natural forces take precedence over human control is immensely satisfying.

The Bay du Nord is a memorial to the fact that we share this land with many other forms of life and that we do not have an inherent right to subdue all of it. As we change other areas in our drive for economic improvement, the Bay du Nord will serve as a stable insurance policy. Our ungainly actions will not be felt within it. It will be one touchstone where we will be able to gain insight into the way it once was.

Few are able to recognize the significance of this event now, but in time, the establishment of the Bay du Nord Wilderness Area will be known as one of this Province's most momentous achievements in nature conservation. It did not happen by default. Many people vigorously pursued the vision for many years.

The Bay du Nord marks a beginning, not an end. It demonstrates a willingness of people to give nature some breathing room. But in itself, it is not enough. More areas where nature will remain unaltered are needed before we can feel that our ecological insurance policy provides adequate coverage.

When I'm eighty, I hope I can look back and see that we took the correct path in setting aside, for all time, the places that best represent our precious natural heritage.

— Caribou and the Avalon —

Twenty-five years ago it would have taken a seasoned countryman many days of tracking to find the one hundred or so caribou remaining in the Avalon caribou herd. Some people would have bet that they were gone all together. Now, in the gently rolling barrens of the Avalon Wilderness Area, over 5,000 animals enjoy some of the lushest caribou range in North America. Only fifty or so kilometres from downtown St. John's, stags engage in fierce, wrenching combat, tearing up the ground in a terrible display of antler, muscle and hoof to establish and maintain a harem of does. A few more leagues to the southeast in a secluded grove of woods, the does bear wobbly calves which take only a few hours to better the speed and grace of human racers. Later in the summer, thousands of does, calves and stags can be found together along either side of the Peter's River Road—a site unrivaled in North America for accessibility and sheer ecological wonder. These are among the biggest and fittest caribou in the world. What a privilege it is to live in this place!

— Geese —

One wintry sunrise, the ground scrunched underfoot as I made my way along the trail. The feathery frost clinging to the brittle fir needles and tendrils of grass floated like fairy dust when I brushed against it. I could almost hear it tinkle. Down on a pond, like scattered curling stones waiting for the start of the games, the geese lay abreast the ice, their feet warmly stowed within their downy plumage.

— November Crossroads —

Fall peters out in November. Winter feels near. The land turns from brilliant reds and yellows to somber hues. Textures replace colour. Storm windows, wood for the fire, and reflections. I think more about where I am and where I'm going in November than at any other time. Compared to November thoughts, New Year's resolutions seem shallow. Grey seas reinforce the power of the natural world and remind me of the short time we have to leave some record of our existence. As my son plays on the floor near me on a cold Sunday evening, I am reminded that our most significant record is in the type of people our children become. I'm content with that. My family is my womb in November.

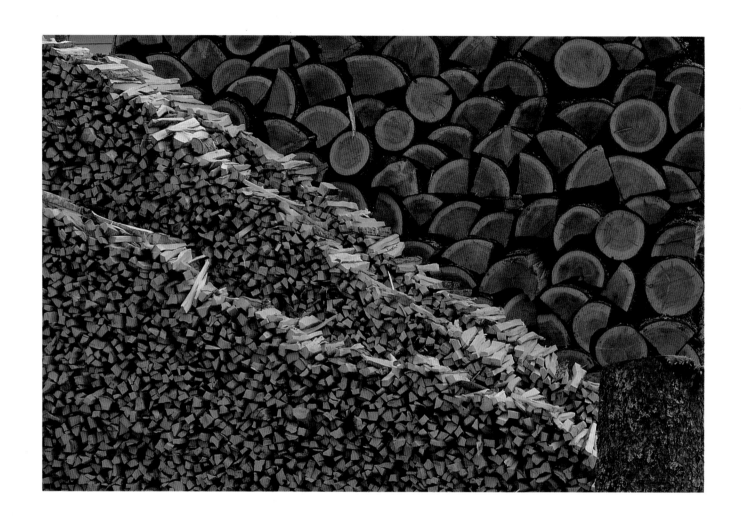